MW00834208

How to Share What You've Made

Practical inspiration to help you stop making excuses, beat your fears and get your book, business or creative project out into the world

Robbie Swale

Winds of Trust Publications

Contents

If you want your work to make a difference,
you can't keep it to yourself. You have to share it.

'In the eyes of those who anxiously seek perfection,
a work is never truly completed, [it is] abandoned.'

– Paul Valéry

Impact

'Robbie will get an acknowledgment in my second book, as he did in my first. The second couldn't have been written without the first and my first would never have been written without Robbie's leadership and his 12-Minute Method. His fingerprints are for evermore on anything I publish! Robbie's guidance will support your progress and will lead you to share the 12-Minute Method with others. It's that good.'

David W. Reynolds
Creator and Host of the Lead. Learn. Change. Podcast;
Author, Lead. Learn. Change

'Robbie's writing and 12-Minute Method inspired me to finally take the first steps to start a business I'd had in my mind (and done nothing about) for years. Learning to lean into Resistance and just take the first step has had a huge impact on my mindset, mental health, family and career development. In the four years since, we have become a successful, award-winning business! I'm extremely grateful to Robbie for his genuinely impactful and thought-provoking 12-minute articles.'

Paul Thompson
Founder/Health and Wellbeing Coach and Consultant,
WorkSmart Wellbeing

'I would highly recommend Robbie to anyone who is facing what feels like an insurmountable hurdle, whether it's personal or professional.'

Emma Kerr
Senior Global Practice Specialist, DAI

'As a true believer in the power of creativity to fire us up and get us into action, I see Robbie as a real leader in the field. His ability to excite and inspire even the most reluctant participants is really impressive. Whether in academia, tech, finance, culture or anything in between, Robbie will help you put aside the noise and focus on what is really important to you.'

Jo Hunter
Co-Founder and CEO, 64 Million Artists

'I wouldn't have written any of what I have without Robbie's example and his 12-minute approach. It's what gave me the initial courage to try such a writing practice myself, to break through both fear and creative blockage…and then to post one article, then several, then to become known for such writing. When someone mentioned I should write a book, the only thing that gave me the confidence to believe I could was seeing what Robbie had already accomplished. I am on page 316 of my flash draft.'

Peter Tavernise
Climate Impact and Regeneration Lead, Cisco

'The ethos of the 12-Minute Method is inspiring and challenging, but it is hearing what led Robbie to it in the first place that connects most. Words matter, but so does the spirit and story behind the words, and that's what catches me more than anything about Robbie's writing.'

Dr Hannah Mather
Executive Coach, Theologian, and Author, The Interpreting Spirit

'I was paralysed by fear and indecision until I came across Robbie's work. Now, thanks to the 12-Minute Method, I believe that I am an author and I am writing my first book.'

Nadine Kelly, M.D.
Founder of NPK Health Integration

'Many times, in many ways, I have recommended the 12-Minute Method to others and watched them come alive with inspiration when they hear how Robbie brought this book to life. His genius ideas are exponentially valuable. To me, it's the 12-Minute Miracle.'

Michelle C. Basey
Energy Healing Artist and CoreYou Coach

'Each time I talk with Robbie, he gives me a new thought to think about.'

Robert Holden
Author, Authentic Success

'"Surely I can find 12 minutes in a day," I thought when I saw Robbie's workshop on how to write a book in 12 minutes. It was a low barrier to entry towards creating a sustainable writing practice. It was the best decision I have made. I have now published a book and have been writing for 483 consecutive days. I would not have done that had it not been for Robbie's idea, but more importantly seeing him walk his talk with the 12-Minute Method.'

Karena de Souza
Author, Contours of Courageous Parenting

'I've always liked to write. However, I'm not a writer. Why would I write, if I'm not a writer? Stumbling upon Robbie's 12-Minute Method gave me permission to write. Anyone can be a writer for 12 minutes! Since incorporating the method into my weekly routine, and publishing on social, I am considered by many to be a "thought leader" in my space.'

Bryon Howard
CEO, The Howard Team Real Estate Services – eXp Realty

'Whatever progress you wish you could make in your career, or more generally in your life – whether it's starting a business, writing your first book, or any other new beginning – Robbie's 12-Minute Method will help you overcome the obstacles in your way, focus your energy and start!'

Alex Swallow
Author, How To Become An Influencer

About the Author

Written on 13th October 2021

I'm Robbie Swale, a writer and coach.

There have been many times in my life where I didn't get my ideas off the ground, where I was stuck in creative hell and where I wasn't productive. Where I didn't share the things I'd made. Thankfully, mostly that has changed.

Now people call me prolific and that's all down to the lessons I learned while creating the 12-Minute Method. Some of the things I have beaten procrastination to do and get out into the world include:

- A blog, clocking in at over 250 articles; each written in 12 minutes

- A coaching business, built from nothing, that could support me full-time in less than two years

- *Aprendiendo español* (I've got a long way to go, but I've been keeping going for more than four years now)

- A website dedicated to my favourite author, now containing over 350 inspirational snippets of wisdom (read more at **www.wisdomofgemmell.com**)

- Two podcasts, The Coach's Journey and The 12-Minute Method, including interviews with best-selling authors and world-famous coaches

- Books: four out now including this one, and another that's almost finished
- A career change
- Getting married

Learn more about how I did all these things by listening to The 12-Minute Method Podcast wherever you get your podcasts.

I spent the first decade of my career doing lots of different things. I was a director, a trustee, a manager, almost a professional actor, a leader and an administrator.

In my current work, I'm interested in three things:

Creativity: (and why people don't do the things they want to do). That's where this book and the 12-Minute Method Series fit in.

Leadership: and how people can be honourable in their work while achieving great things. How they can find success without feeling like they have to compromise their values and identity.

Coaching: the amazing craft that allows each of us to develop vital skills for our future, to more often be our wisest and most skilful selves, and to move closer to fulfilling our potential.

I've coached people working on amazing creative ideas, from businesses to books and beyond. I've worked with people on many incredible projects that you will never have heard of. I've also worked, coached, trained and facilitated for organisations like Deutsche Bank, the University of Edinburgh, the Royal Opera House, Moonpig, UCL and more.

I'm proud to be an associate of 64 Million Artists, an organisation dedicated to unleashing the creativity of everyone in the UK, and a Fellow Coach for BetterUp, the world's biggest mental health and coaching organisation.

Mostly, though, I'm proud that I've felt fear, felt Resistance, felt the pull of procrastination, and I've battled it, knowing that that battle was a battle for my soul: to take me out of creative hell and grow me into someone new. There have been many ideas that haven't made it out into the world because I didn't know how to fight that battle. But my line is drawn: *not anymore.*

Read more about me and sign up to my mailing list at

www.robbieswale.com

About This Book

The aim of this book is clear.

It's for you if you're hesitating to share something you have made, no matter how large or small. From a book you've written, to a business you're ready to launch, to a joke on Facebook, this book is here to help you take that final and often most fear-filled step.

And share it.

Like the first two books in the series (and a little like the third), this isn't a how-to in the traditional sense. You won't get six easy steps to share your work. You'll get a series of ideas that might help you. They might not all help you, but at least one of them will.

I don't think you'd be here if you didn't want to share your work, or share yourself, more. So my invitation to you is this:

Read this book looking for that one piece of practical inspiration that might take you from being someone who has made something to being someone who has shared it. It might come from how this book was written, or in an insight or idea in one of the chapters.

It might be in this section. I might have already said it.

The aim, in the end, is to be courageous enough to share something even when it scares you to do that. In fact, that's my definition of courage: acting in the face of fear. My aim for this book is to inspire that courage in you.

You might find the one insight, the one moment of inspiration anywhere, and your task is to read this book in whatever way is most likely to give you that inspiration.

You can dip in, skip to the end, read whatever catches your eye. Permission to do any of those things and more, granted.

Permission to just go and share your work now, granted. Go do it. See what happens. If you can feel the courage now, then go do it and come back to this book later, when it seems harder.

And, permission to read start-to-finish. This isn't a long book. That's strange to me, given that my writing practice was essentially an experiment for me to get over my fear of sharing myself and my work.

But in some way that's probably because the message of sharing is clear in *how* the book was written, in how my writing evolved. More on that shortly.

There isn't just one way to get around our procrastination on sharing, and there isn't just one place we procrastinate. Maybe one idea in the book will help you today, maybe another will help you tomorrow.

Read looking for them.

And when you find the insights, the ones that might help you share your work now or later, you might want to make a note of them. If you do, and want somewhere to record them, I've created a free worksheet to help with that. It also guides you through how to create your own 12-minute practice. You can download the worksheet and some other little gifts here:

www.robbieswale.com/12minute-method-downloads

There are many sensible-seeming reasons to keep your head down in the world, to not share your work and to not take the courageous steps that you – given you're here – almost certainly want to take.

I hope that through this book you'll see why those sensible-seeming reasons should be ignored. And that you'll see that there are very important reasons for you to share your work.

Connect to those reasons as you read. For you, they're probably connected to the reasons that you started making your work or thinking about your book, business or creative project in the first place.

Or they may be about what you see around you in your life, and your desire to make a contribution to a better world.

Or they may be about something different.

From everything I've experienced when helping people take the steps they want to take, and to create and share the things that are calling them, I feel very confident that whatever it is you are making will make a difference. These things that really matter to us always seem to make a positive difference, for us and others.

So choose your own adventure with this book. Use it in whatever way will help you get your work out there.

If that's a reminder on your bookshelf or bedside table, perfect.

If it's as a doorstop, so that every time you wedge open your kitchen door you remember to share your work, perfect.

If it's by reading this and then getting up and doing something courageous...perfect.

The world is changed when people take courageous steps to change it.

Use this book to help you do that.

Robbie Swale
16th September, 2022

The 12-Minute Method

Written on 16th September 2022

And so here we are, at the beginning of the end of this series of four books. You don't need to have read the other three to read this one. But it feels important to acknowledge that this is the final part, because it is also, really, where it all started.

So much has come from a phrase uttered in a coaching session.

Something about 'sharing myself'.

That phrase was there in the coaching session because of the stress and anxiety that sharing myself, including via things I had made, seemed to cause me.

And yet, along with my coach, Joel Monk, I faced it head on.

As I remember it, it wasn't then about being creative, as it is now. In fact, it's only relatively recently that I have really accepted that I am a creative person, strange as that may seem to some people who know me.

At the time, it was about this pain I had; a pain I now call 'creative hell' – the pain of wanting to do something but being wrapped in so much procrastination, worry and doubt that I didn't do it.

I haven't always been like that, but in 2016, I was. It would show up even when making jokes on Facebook, let alone launching my coaching business. Let alone creating a website about my favourite author. Let alone writing something.

While speaking to Raquel Ark about my journey as a coach for an episode of my podcast, The Coach's Journey, I found myself saying: I was scared.

And I was. Because really, underneath the procrastination, worry and doubt, is fear. Fear of so many things, many of them scarier when allowed to be vague clouds of fear in the back of my mind than when seen in the cold light of day. But I was, without doubt, scared.

Joel and I faced it because that's what you sometimes do in coaching. We faced it because Joel heard something when I talked about sharing myself that touched something in him. We faced it because I knew that being able to share things online would be really useful if I wanted to make a success of my coaching business, and that that would be a lot harder if it always felt as hard as this.

And we faced it because of Steven Pressfield.

His book, *The War of Art*, had already been important to me. In it, Pressfield describes the universal force of Resistance, which tries to stop us doing what matters to us, and he outlines strategies to deal with it. I had already found the ideas in there useful in getting my business started, in talking about my work more, in getting *The Wisdom of David Gemmell* (**www.wisdomofgemmell.com**) off the ground. And among many powerful ideas in that book is a rule of thumb: 'The more important a call or action is to our soul's evolution, the more Resistance we will feel towards pursuing it.'

We partly, I suspect, faced down this fear of sharing things and all the Resistance that was there because I'd read that rule of thumb and I'd felt the truth in it.

And given what has happened since, there is no doubt that facing down those fears and sharing my work has been every bit as important to my growth and evolution as it was challenging at the start.

Joel and I worked on this. I shared a poem online. I wrote an article, prompted by Joel's coaching. And then came the key moment, which will be etched in my story forever more.

Joel explained that when he was a visual artist earlier in his career, he liked to create series of paintings. What if I created a series of articles?

We had already talked about, and maybe used, my short train journey from Clapham Junction to London Waterloo as a window for creativity. Somehow, while on the train I was free; free from the pressures of getting somewhere or doing something or maximising my time. It was spare, spacious. I could use it for reading, or listening to a podcast. Or, perhaps, for the two weeks that followed, I could use it for writing.

Here's what we came up with: write five articles over the next two weeks. The practice was this: write while the train is moving, stop when it stops, proofread it once with tiny edits and post it online.

I would post it on LinkedIn ('No one reads LinkedIn' I thought). And then we would see.

What we saw was this: none of my fears of what would happen if I shared some part of myself came true. No one laughed at me. No one mocked me. No one said I was wrong, or picked holes in my writing or my ideas. I wasn't humiliated. I wasn't thrown out of the tribe. I wasn't alone and starving somewhere.

Instead, when I got responses (and there weren't many on those early articles), people liked them.

And, more importantly, I knew something was up. It wasn't *fun* to post them – the pain and worry while hovering over the post button was there, although diluted by the way the practice was designed (if you tell everyone it was written on the train with one proofread, then the pressure definitely comes off a bit). But I could tell it was a good thing for me to be doing it. Now I reflect that what I felt was the power of acting in the face of fear; that is, the power of courage.

So I turned The Train Series into a weekly practice. Once a week, write an article on the train and post it online. That was August 2016, so as I write this I have now been doing that every week for more than six years.

Six years of sharing something I have made, every week.

As time went on and my business grew I left the part-time job I had in 2016, and so commuted into London less frequently. I needed a way to keep the practice going, so one day I checked how long the journey took me. It took 12 minutes. So, in the weeks I wasn't commuting into London I would set a timer for 12 minutes, write while the timer was going, stop when it stopped, proofread it once and post it online.

Gradually, the train blog became the 12-minute blog. And, in the end, The 12-Minute Method.

And that 12-Minute Method has transformed me. It has changed me into someone who can – as I might have hoped in 2016 – share the things they have made online without the out-of-proportion knots of fear and worry. Not without any fear or worry, I should say. I still feel it, I still worry; I'm still scared sometimes. But not like I used to be. And it doesn't stop me anymore. Because I know it's part of the game.

But that isn't the end of the 12-Minute Method story. In 2019, I had the thought of making my blog into a book.

I was inspired a little by marketing thought-leader Seth Godin publishing a book of his blog. And I also used one of the tricks I use to get myself into action. Later in this book you'll read about how if even *one person* is impacted by your work, then it matters that you make it.

I realised that if there was someone who really wanted to read all my blogs, they would find it really hard. And, as I'll write again later, they might be the most important person – the person I can change the most, the person who counts. LinkedIn wasn't made to show people an archive of blog posts. A book could do that, though. And although I thought 'who am I to publish a book?', I used my trick: it's not about me. It's about the person who might love to read it. And I won't know who that is or what impact it has until I've made the book.

Plus, I thought, I could call it *I Wrote This Book in 12 Minutes*, which amused me.

I enlisted help to make this book and sat down with my friend Steve in Doppio Coffee in Battersea to talk about it. He asked an important question. He said something like: 'It's a great title. But can the book itself do what the title does?'

The title said: I wrote a book in 12 minutes a week for three years. What excuse do you have for not doing the thing YOU want to do?

But could what happens inside the book help people to face that same challenge?

I didn't know. So I set out to find out.

I spoke to my coach at the time, Katie Harvey, and thought through the phases required to make something that matters. I came up with four.

Then I printed off three years of blogs. There were about 140 of them and 80,000 words. Read that again. It's still amazing. 12 minutes, every week (apart from holidays) for three years. That got me 80,000 words.

I dealt out the blog posts into the four piles and remarkably, they pretty much all found a home. There were a few that didn't, but remarkably few, and remarkably few that overlapped so much that there wasn't any point in including both versions. You can read those articles, the ones that didn't make it, in the short eBook *The Cutting Room*, available at **www.robbieswale.com/12minute-method-downloads**

But the rest, they fitted with those four stages.

This surprised me: I had written a book *about something*. But it shouldn't have surprised me really.

Writing in 12 minutes necessarily – and importantly – removes my chance to think about what I'm writing. Procrastination happens in the head, so getting your head out of the way is a good move. All I had time to think about, really, is: what am I interested in this week?

And what I was interested in was people struggling to do the things they wanted to do. That's what had been happening in my life: I'd been wrestling with myself to launch a business, grow, learn, write and share my work.

I'd had to face down so many parts of myself to do that.

And I'd been coaching people. And what is coaching, really, except helping people do the things they want to do, that they haven't done yet?

So really, it shouldn't be a surprise that I'd written about that. But it was. Not just any 80,000 words. But 80,000 words about something. About creativity, procrastination, Resistance and finally doing these things that really matter to us.

80,000 words about how to move from creative hell into being the kind of person who makes a difference – makes the biggest difference they can – by making work and then sharing it.

In the end, I decided that to make the work as accessible as possible, it would be a series of four shorter books, not one longer one. And that's when the 12-Minute Method series was born.

And so the 12-Minute Method is two things.

The 12-Minute Method is: sit down, every week, for just enough time, and work on what matters. That is what led me to the incredibly obvious insight that I just hadn't appreciated until these books began to take shape. The insight is this:

If you do something, even something small, every week and you don't stop, in the end you might end up with something magical.

And The 12-Minute Method is a four-step process, the four stages I identified. What would have been the four parts of *I Wrote This Book in 12 Minutes*. The four books in the 12-Minute Method series.

To make work that matters, here's what you have to do:

1. Start. Everything that was made by a person at some point was started. So, first, make sure to start. That's what *How to Start When You're Stuck* is about.

2. Keep going. Don't give up. If we start something and we keep going then almost anything becomes possible, if we give ourselves a long enough timeframe. If we know we won't give up, and we keep making the time, then in the end what we want to get done will get done. That's what *How to Keep Going When You Want to Give Up* is about.

3. Create the conditions for great work. Great work of any kind is too complex for us to 'make it happen'. The best we can do is to enable it, is to help it happen, is to make ourselves almost accidentally prone to doing it. That's the third book in the series, *How to Create the Conditions For Great Work*.

4. Share it. That's the last part. If we want our work to make a difference beyond ourselves, we have to share it. And if we want to do our part in making tomorrow's world better than today's, we have to make a difference beyond ourselves. That's what this book is about.

It's important to say that although it makes most sense to have Share come last when you're making a series of books, sharing our work (no matter what it is like) is far more important than creating the conditions for great work, or waiting until we've created those conditions before we share what we've made. So many great projects have been lost in the procrastination of 'creating the conditions for great work'.

The most important thing for your project is that you start. The next most important is that you don't give up. And the next most important is that you share it.

Once you've done that, and practised doing that, *then* it's a good time to start thinking about fulfilling your potential, about how to do even better work. About creating the conditions for the genius inside you – and you do have genius inside you – to emerge.

Because no great work happens unless people start and keep going.

And no work is truly great unless it's shared.

The novelist Toni Morrison said: 'If there's a book you really want to read, but it hasn't been written yet, then you must write it.'

And whilst I didn't do it quite that much through choice, this is absolutely a book for me. And it's for you, if you're a perfectionist or a procrastinator or someone whose fear has held them back from releasing what they could be into the world.

That's why this book isn't called 'Finish'. That's why I included that Paul Valéry quote in the opening pages. At some point, we have to call time on the 'finishing' process. We have to abandon what we have made and share it.

It won't be perfect. And I've needed these books at every stage of publishing them. I've needed all the lessons in here to help make sure I share these things, so that they have the chance to do the work that they can do.

'This book is too short', 'There's not enough content', 'It doesn't cover *all* the important things about sharing'.

Imperfect it most certainly is. But then, so is everything.

In this book you'll find a selection of the 12-minute articles – the ones that are about ensuring you make the courageous decisions to share your work and yourself.

At the end, in the final chapter, you'll find something written in the same period and in one sitting, but not in 12 minutes. Although it is longer, it absolutely belongs here in this book and in this series.

And so now is the time. The time to start sharing, or sharing more.

Over the last few years, as I have thought about my work, I have been lucky to be provoked to deep insight by many people: mentors, coaches, clients, family and friends. One of them, Robert Holden, prompted me with questions of purpose. And what emerged for me, not from thought but from nowhere, was this:

The shared purpose of humanity is to create the kingdom of heaven on earth.

Whether you are religious or not – and I am not, really – we need those kinds of words to talk about the scale of the possibility and the problems.

As I reflected on that purpose, I came to see something.

This work – the work of helping people finally do the things they have wanted and been meaning to do for weeks, months, years, even decades – is the work of that purpose. This is for two reasons.

The first is the feeling of not doing these things that call us. That feeling is hell. And so if anyone reading this takes the steps of courage required to share their work and themselves, then in one person's mind, at least, we have tilted towards heaven and away from hell.

The second is that I have spoken to many people about the things that they, deep down, want to create. And no one yet has told me an idea or a possibility that doesn't move the world towards the good, the true or the beautiful. That is, away from hell and towards heaven.

Your idea, whether it is a book, a business, some other creative project, a change in you, a change in your organisation, or a change in your family, will do that.

Doing it will show you who you can be when you act with courage. Will show you the possibilities before you to change things, in yourself and the world.

Doing it will change who you are and take you out of that creative hell. At least out of some of it – there may still be more tasks to do.

And, if you share it, then you will change the world, too. At the very least, you may change one person's world. And that's something.

We will never know, when we share something, if it will disappear into the ether without a trace or transform the world more than we could imagine. We can't know that for sure before we share it.

But that shouldn't stop us.

If you want to do your bit to tilt the world towards heaven, and away from hell, then now's the time.

Make something that counts.

And then share it.

Free 12-Minute Method Action Sheet

I want you to use this book to help you share what you've made. And so I've created a worksheet that guides you through creating your own 12-minute practice and gives you somewhere to turn the insights you get from this book into action.

It also includes some recommended further reading from the thinkers and authors who have influenced this book and the rest of the series, whose names you'll find in the chapters that follow.

You can download the action sheet for free at
www.robbieswale.com/12minute-method-downloads
or by scanning this QR code:

Chapter One

Let Yourself Out Into The World

Written on 29th November, 2016

Here's an idea: let yourself out into the world.

Not just any you, but the you underneath.

The one hidden by expectations, by pressure, by what you think other people think. By what you thought someone thought you should think, long ago. The one clouded by tactics and strategies and winning. And losing.

That's where the magic is. It's underneath all that.

It came to me today in a session with my coach. These sessions often or always contain magic but this was one of the moments that has had the most profound effect on me. After it, my friend Nicole Brigandi said that she thought I was floating, and tried to tread on the corner of the magic carpet carrying me.

And that's what she saw, some kind of shift. The kind of shift that is at once instantaneous and the product of months and months of work.

This piece is about letting myself out into the world. This whole series is. That's where it comes from. What could I do that is about creativity, and not about the pressures of trying to grow my business? I could write an article. But there was too much pressure on that. I could write it on LinkedIn, which no one reads anyway. But still... I could write it and post it straight away. But there was still too much opportunity for Resistance to get the better of me there. I could write an article on my train journey and post it with (almost) no edits, as soon as I can.

In that practice there is very little space for things to get in the way: no time for Resistance, or expectations, or nerves, or tactics, or what I think someone thought I should think, many years ago. There's just me.

And it's that me that led to the opportunities that now beckon, as part of this journey to find the things I am good at, the things I love doing, and the contribution I want to make to the world. That journey has been about understanding me, and finding the places where I can let myself out into the world.

I found some of that at The Coaching School. My friend Sarah Dawrant described being part of a Coaching School group as being like leaving the house without a jacket and the temperature being the same inside and outside. No need for any jackets to distract you there. You just need to let yourself out into the world.

And I've continued to do that more and more ever since I studied there, and before, too. Last week Nicole and I did a talk to about a hundred people about personal branding. Our main message was: Be Yourself. Be You.[1]

Being yourself can sound hard. It isn't easy. We aren't used to doing it.

But try this: let yourself out into the world. It doesn't have to be in a big way. But let yourself out. A little bit. Today.

Note

1   You can watch that talk in full here: https://www.youtube.com/watch?v=MMLjgujjAxY or by searching 'Mastering your personal brand' on YouTube.

Chapter Two

Show Us What Your Wonderful Soul Can Create

Written on 18th September, 2017

Resistance has been kicking my ass recently.

Last month I ran a seminar on Resistance, and as part of that I realised and then shared with the group that I needed to turn pro with my writing. Turning pro is Steven Pressfield's language for how to beat Resistance. It basically means I need to knuckle down. First step, schedule some writing time in my diary. I had two hours for it this morning. I probably managed about 45 minutes of actual writing. I started five minutes late and faffed around with wondering what to write for most of the next 45 minutes. Then I started writing, then my fiancée came home from a medical appointment after 45 more minutes and I spent time talking with her and having lunch. All important things, all stopping me from writing.

I settled on working to finish something I'd already started: I have about 11,000 words of what might be a short book about the struggle to live life from a place of possibility, not one of lack and scarcity. I wrote most of it about a year ago. And since then it has been sitting, unfinished. Almost untouched.[2]

And Resistance was doing its work on me as I tried to write. In all sorts of ways. I was questioning whether it should be something else that I should be writing about with my writing time, not this 'book'. I was questioning who am I to write about relationships and politics, and more importantly: who am I to draw together a set of concepts and say 'this is a way to make your life better'?

And the answer is another question: who am I not to?

Who am I to say what people will or won't find valuable? Who am I to deny the world the thoughts and ideas that I have found useful? If only one person finds a way, through those thousands of words, to live a happier, healthier life, isn't that worth it?

And that's one of the worst things about the irresistible universal force, Resistance, the set of concepts and ideas that Steven Pressfield draws together. It leaves all sorts of almost finished ideas and art gathering dust as relics of another time. We have all had them. A business idea never pursued. A song unfinished or unshared. A passion not fulfilled.

What if each of us could have improved the life of just one person by sharing that art, those ideas? If each of us could have done that, then billions of people would be happier, healthier and more fulfilled than they are now.

And here's the secret: I can guarantee that sharing that creativity would have improved the life of one person. It would have improved the life of the sharer. The reason I know that is that creativity, making something from nothing, whether that is one of the traditional arts, or a website, or a business, or just something that you're holding inside, shows us something magical. It shows us we can do things. We can make things. We can change things. It gives us hope.

And here's one last thing. The chances are, you're some of the way there already. There's a version of my part-finished book in each of you somewhere, and it probably doesn't take that much to finish it. But the longer you wait, the harder it will be, especially if you listen to Resistance.

Remember, the answer mostly comes in knuckling down. Choose a dusty piece of your art, unshared or unfinished, and answer this question: what's the biggest amount of time you can give to it this week? Then give it that time, or as much of it as your Resistance will let you. Then share it. If you can't bring yourself to share it with the world, share it with a friend, someone who understands this stuff. If you don't have a friend like that, share it with me.

I'd love to see it. It might make all the difference to me.

I'd love to see what your wonderful soul can create. And so would the world.

Note

2   At the time of publishing How to Share What You've Made, the book I mention in this chapter is still not out. It is now a lot longer and provisionally titled The Power to Choose, and you can read a draft version of the first half on my website, here: https://www.robbieswale.com/writing/2020/3/23/why-am-i-sharing-parts-of-my-forthcoming-book-the-power-to-choose

Chapter Three

The Fear Of Exposure

Written on 17th November, 2016

The fear of being exposed is deep in many of us.

Many of my most powerful childhood memories are of finding myself exposed in different ways. People laughing at me. Me not knowing what the 'right thing to do' was.

Last night, I felt a powerful emotional reaction to a memory of a situation. The situation, which came to me while coaching someone about creating connection with others, involved meeting someone and knowing them. In the memory, I wanted the connection we had to continue, beyond the perhaps time-limited relationship we had. But I was afraid to say that. I was afraid to ask. I was afraid to reach out in case that person didn't reciprocate. Then I'd be exposed. I'd be there, by myself, heart on my sleeve, saying: 'I want to connect.' Someone else would be saying: 'I don't.'

The strong feeling that took me over as I reflected on this situation was an intense gratitude for another memory: of when someone who I wanted to connect with – but was too afraid to reach out to – reached out to me. When someone else risked exposure to say to me: 'I'd like to connect with you.' And I could say: 'Wow, me too.'

In my adult life, I've become better at this. I am better at offering myself in those situations. But it's still hard. There's still a strong resistance to exposure. The fear of rejection. The fear of being out there, exposed, on a mountainside in a storm. Left there by someone who could have taken you in, who could have connected. Left there by someone to whom you said: 'Here I am. I'm offering to you, in my vulnerability, a part of myself. Share it with me.'

But they don't always leave you there. And in our modern world it's rarely actually a mountainside in a storm. And when we find the connection, in that sharing is love.

Chapter Four

The Fear Of Exposure II

Written on 25th November, 2016

The fear of exposure is about putting yourself out there, offering connection to people. Being willing to say 'here I am'.

There are many ways we hide from this risk, linked to primal fears of being thrown out into the dangers of the wilderness. Here's another one.

We hide in the language we use. We hide what we really think.

I do it, and it was brought into the light by a reflection from my coach, Joel Monk. He pointed out that, after I have answered a question or spoken about something that is important to me, I sometimes finish the sentence with a kind of vocal tick.

I answer a question, and in my coaching this is often a question about what I want, the future I want to create, or how I see the world, what is really important to me. Thinking back now I can hear the conviction in my voice, and the truth in what I'm saying. And then I end the paragraph, the speech, with a phrase like:

'Or something like that.'

'Maybe...'

'Or at least, I think that's it.'

Joel asked me: 'What's that about?'

And the answer is quite clear. I'm hiding. I'm afraid. I'm afraid that if people know what I really think, then... Well, then I don't know what will happen. They might hate what I think and then hate me. They might want to kick me out of the tribe.

I want to be loved, like everyone does. So it's safer not to risk anything.

But what about the people who might be changed by our conviction? Who we might connect with, if they could really feel the core of us, unobstructed by our distraction tactics? And how will we change if we lean into the message that is coming out of us and let it come?

Where are you hiding?

Chapter Five

The Three Types Of Sharing

Written on 6ᵗʰ June, 2018

I was speaking to a client a few months ago about sharing. Because there are different types of sharing, and they come from and lead to very different things.

We have just finished working together, after six months of work, and as preparation for that I read through the notes from our work and came across that conversation about sharing. And it felt pertinent, as I am wrestling with my own ability to share: to try to understand that my sharing with others is okay. Deep, personal sharing; asking for help. It isn't taking up the space from others who need the help more than me. And it isn't too much for people.

This is the age of sharing: a 'share' button at the bottom of every page, success for many people based on how many 'shares' they get, and our ability to share, in so many ways, easier and with fewer gatekeepers than ever before. And that, as with everything, has a light side and a shadow.

Here are some of the types of sharing I see in the world.

Sharing for the ego: In this space, we are sharing to let everyone else know what is going on, hoping that they do something. Sometimes this is to celebrate, sometimes to commiserate. Some people share a short, cryptic statement, with their ego desperate to be heard, to have people sympathise, or to have its stories corroborated. This isn't all bad – it's lovely that we can share the things we want to with our family and loved ones and those we know or are connected to. And it's important that our ego gets what it needs to keep us safe and sane. But sharing for the ego doesn't help us with everything. And in some cases, it's not helpful at all.

Sharing for our own healing: Sometimes we are in pain. And we need to share it. Sharing relieves that pain sometimes, dissipates it somehow. Sometimes we just need to know other people are out there and the reactions of people – in real life or online – are a balm to keep us in place, to keep us going. We need people in our lives who we can do that with. And, as my brother Ewan Townhead once wrote beautifully, they need to be someone who can handle it.

Sometimes, you just know that you need to share, for the good of your soul. It isn't from a place of pain in the now, mostly, but it may be from a place of pain in the past. If we find the way to do that, to share in those moments, then the connection with others that sharing brings can be incredibly powerful. It doesn't heal everything, but the vulnerability it takes and the power of being accepted for who we are, including what we shared, can be a deeply human experience. People may not know this is what you are doing. I doubt the readers of my first few posts in this series knew that I was sharing them in order to heal myself of some scar that brought on an irrational terror of sharing in that way, and that their acceptance had healed something.

That is how this practice started, although it has become something more than that, now – perhaps a combination of these three types of sharing.

Sharing for others' healing: This is the third type of sharing. Because hearing about the true, authentic experiences of others can be incredibly healing. We spend so much time comparing our internal experiences to others' external experiences that the comparison trap can cause us a lot of pain. To truly hear from others is a powerful gift and can empower us and even heal our scars and wounds.

So share, when you can. Share more than you think. And remember what a powerful impact it can have for you, and for others.

For each of us, the challenges are different. These days, my practices mean I've got some of my sharing needs sorted. I've got some good stuff down around sharing for others and my sharing for my ego does ok, too. But sharing for myself? For me, that's the real edge.

Chapter Six

The Lost Relics Of Our Art

Written on 8th February, 2018

On my computer is a folder. It contains more than 20 Word documents, each with a set of lyrics and a set of chords. They are songs, written with care and a sprinkling of pain, in my late teens and early 20s. In my late 20s I came back to them in a moment of loneliness. As I came back to myself in that loneliness and struggle, I came back to the music. It had been such a part of me, but I had left it behind and I could feel that leaving that creativity behind wasn't quite me.

I played two of those songs live to a crowd of 100 people. And I felt the connection to those pieces of art and I didn't want them to disappear forever. So I reached out to a friend, to ask if he would help me create something from them. Not from all of them, but from the best of them. He couldn't do it, because he was in too challenging a place in his own life. He didn't feel he could do them justice. And then, for me, the time had passed. Because they aren't all that special, and my voice is not so good. And if I recorded them, I would want to do them real justice. And so those songs sit there, in Word documents, on my computer. Lost relics of art. Unshared.

Noel Gallagher, in the rush of creativity from leaving behind his band, Oasis, which had become restrictive to his creativity, produced two albums at once. He released the first album, with the second due to follow six months later. But by the time six months passed, he felt the time for those songs had passed, or perhaps they weren't quite right, and so the album was never released. Maybe some of those songs have resurfaced in his two subsequent albums but I suspect at least some of them haven't. They just sit there, on some hard disk somewhere. Lost relics of art. Unshared.

Creativity shows up for each of us in different ways. We don't all have a pile of songs or poems hidden away somewhere (although I suspect far more of us do than we realise). For others it will be a business idea, perhaps a list of them. Unrealised. It might be 1,000 or 10,000 photographs on a hard disk. Unshared. It might be five ideas, designed in the pub on a Friday with colleagues, to shift the culture of your organisation to one that it would delight you to be part of. Unavailable, still, to you and to the people around you, whose work might be changed by them.

If there is one thing I have learnt from 18 months of posting a short post, like this one, written in 12 minutes, once a week, it is that my skill at predicting how useful a piece of my writing will be to others is poor. No matter how much I have doubted the point of posting an article, people get in touch with me and tell me they have read it, and they have liked it, and it made a difference to them. It is important to share, therefore, no matter what I think.

I regret that Noel didn't publish his songs, because so many of his songs over the last 25 years have had such an impact on me. And not just on me: on hundreds of thousands – probably millions – of people. He might be right that these songs weren't good enough. But I want to listen to them. I suspect, one day, someone will dig them out and release them. That is what has been happening with David Gemmell, my favourite author.

After his death, two of his books, one unpublished and one out of print, have been released. Gemmell felt that as they were modern detective stories they didn't fit in with the canon of his work. But it has been wonderful to feel the effect of his magical and soulful writing again. I'm glad these lost relics of his art were found and shared.

But what are the relics that you are not sharing? Who are you to say that they will not deeply affect me? Who are you to say that they will not change the course of the life of someone you love, or someone you have never met?

Return to some of those relics, today if you can. Return with a generosity. See them in the real world. Yes, they may not be as good as the perfection in your mind, but that is part of the nature of art. And, yes, they may be better than your Resistance told you when you created them.

Perhaps you have done the work, already, to create change in the world. Perhaps all you need to do is share it – a small, but not so easy thing to do. But perhaps now, the *You of Today* can see past the doubts from the *You of Yesterday*.

Share it.

Chapter Seven

If You Are Wrong, Admit It And Change

Written on 29th May, 2019

I wrote an article. And, for the first time in almost three years of this practice, I'm not posting it. I'm writing this instead.

I wrote about the flaws in Oxfam's rich list and the incredible Grievance Studies scandal, which seems to cast doubt on the validity of whole sections of our cultural thinking, and when I came back to it to publish it I felt like I couldn't. Because I wasn't sure I was right. Well, I was pretty sure I was right about some of it, most of it, but there was a flaw in the logic – potentially – which meant that if I posted it I might be wrong.

Then, I was stuck in something because the title of the post was going to be *When you realise you're wrong, admit it and change*. And, I was stuck because the work I am doing on myself right now is to be more comfortable speaking about things out in the world. To be more comfortable speaking the truth as I see it. Not to let the people who shout others down and call others out grind me down.

And, I'm always on the journey of outfoxing that old devil, Resistance.

So, what do I do? Do I post the piece, even though I suspect that there's a flaw in my logic and storytelling, even though I think the conclusion I reach is right? That would, after all, give me a chance to live out the aims of the piece, admitting I'm wrong and changing it?

Or do I – given I already suspect that in some ways I am 'wrong' – change it straight away?

And, I'm *someone who writes*. I need to publish something, as part of my practice.

I decided not to share the piece I'd written, and I'm about 90 per cent sure that this isn't Resistance getting me (in the first draft of this piece, I was only 60 per cent sure, but by the time I proof-read it I was up to 90 per cent). This article, it seems as I write this, is about me unpacking why I was right not to share it. I want to speak out more. That's part of my work on myself, and as time goes on I believe more and more that almost all of us need to make that part of our work on ourselves. There do seem to be parts of society, as highlighted by the Grievance Studies scandal, and probably encouraged by the Twittersphere, that shut down our ability to speak about certain things. There are other parts of society, like the people at Rebel Wisdom who organised a summit structured around saying what you feel unable to say, focused on empowering people to speak up.

At the Rebel Wisdom summit, one of the speakers said something that allowed me to drop down even deeper into something I believe to be the truth: that in the complexity of the modern world, where changing one thing slightly can shift everything else and we can't be sure of the impact of the things we do, there is really only *one thing* you can do: that is to do work on yourself, to continue to deepen yourself so that you are aware of all the unique gifts and struggles you have. To become more able to live as what Steven Pressfield might call your Higher Self and what Jordan Hall would call sovereign. As you do that, you can see the truth more clearly and be increasingly sure that the things you are saying come from that higher and deeper part of you. If you don't do that work, then you can't be sure they don't come from your baser parts, your more animal instincts. And then, if things go wrong, it really is your fault. You can't say 'at least I did my best'. Because you didn't.

So we all need to speak up more. And we all need to do work on ourselves, to make sure that when we speak up we are speaking from the deepest wisdom available to us.

But also we have to be careful. We have to be careful because we want to take people with us. And we have to be careful because there seems to be a culture war going on and there is a lot of (sensible) fear that each or any of us may be jumped on for our views, no matter how well-meaning they are.

This practice – the 12-minute article – has limits, and some of them appear when trying to express deeply nuanced ideas. I have got better at that over three years but I am not perfect and I couldn't do it with my last attempt.

I hope I was right to reset the game at that point and press play again with this piece. But I didn't just reset it. Because I'm doing my own work as I press reset. Speak out; share your work and ideas; it's important that you do. But the message of this piece is the same as the message of the other: if you are wrong – even slightly wrong, even in just the way you are telling a story, even when the conclusion is still true – admit it and change.

Chapter Eight

The Marketing Trap I Most Often Fall Into

Written on 16th November, 2018

I tell myself so many strange stories about marketing. Often, the way I try and catch myself is to come back to a story I learned from my brother, Ewan Townhead, in his writing about marketing.

The story goes something like this:

You think that only snake oil salesmen and sleazy internet marketers use internet marketing strategies. So you don't do them. Because you're too good, and pure, and you're not one of those evil, sleazy bastards. Maybe you even sit, sometimes, looking across a room at someone you're pretty sure is using those techniques *right now* on some poor, unsuspecting person. And the person is *taken in by it* and ends up working with the snake oil salesman.

In coaching, I have this feeling about all the adverts I get on Facebook promising to turn my business into a six-/seven-/one-million-figure business in just six easy steps.

But here's the problem. Who are you serving with your high-and-mightiness? With your 'I won't use any marketing techniques because I'm too good and pure'? With your 'real success doesn't come from tricking people into working with you'?

Are you serving yourself? No. *You are letting yourself down.* Because those techniques can be powerful and lots of poor unsuspecting people are buying from a snake oil salesman who then won't even deliver value to them, not like you would if they even knew about you. Which they don't because you refuse to use the techniques.

Are you serving the person buying? God no, *you are letting her down.* Instead of doing some incredibly useful and powerful work with you, she is buying some crappy six-part tool from someone else, which isn't even going to help her.

Are you serving the snake oil salesman? No, *you are letting him down, too.* Because while he gets away with running a crappy business based on snake oil promises, he doesn't have to learn, or grow, or change, or become the person he could be.

So, I remind myself and I remind you: *serve people.* Do what serves people most, even if that is doing 'marketing' or 'sales', which you think is horrible or icky. Remember Rule Number 6 (don't take yourself so god damn seriously!)[3] and get on with it.

I have been remembering this story and trying to remind myself of this all week. I got offered $100 of free advertising credit from LinkedIn. I like free stuff and I like playing with technology. And I've recently relaunched my group programme for coaches, which I'm going to run for the second time in 2019. I first built a following of coaches after an article about my journey to being a full-time coach went mini-viral (it has been read over 7,000 times) and I thought: 'Well, I could put that $100 on that article, and see what happens, and maybe get it out to some more people.' And then I created the advert. And then I sat on it.

The Resistance was funny this time. It was mainly: 'But it got to 7,470 views *on its own*. It got there *organically*. Do I want to *spoil* that by advertising it?'

Wow, remember Rule Number 6, dude.

And then, remember that there's a reason that 7,470 people have clicked on it and you've connected with hundreds of coaches through it. Because it's *good*, because it *served people*. Remember Rule Number 6 and get on with it.

How *dare* I let my bizarre worries about 'purity' get in the way of getting an article that has inspired many in front of even one more person?

The advert will go live on Monday.

I learnt something else this week: apparently if you like your own LinkedIn posts a few days after you share them, they sometimes get a third more views. 'But I can't do that, it's *sad*.' Oh, *dude*. Remember Rule Number 6. Who might you not be serving because someone else might think 'it looks sad'? Get over yourself and like some posts.

This all applies to you, too. Remember Rule Number 6, get on with it and get your work out there. How *dare* you not do it?

Note

3   I first heard the Rule Number 6 story in the powerful book, The Art of Possibility by Rosamund Stone Zander and Ben Zander.

Chapter Nine

You Are Stealing From People By Not Marketing Your Work

Written on 24th July, 2019

We need to bust through our Resistance around marketing, and it was great to get another wake-up call this week and it was this, from marketing guru Seth Godin: **you are stealing from other people if you aren't marketing your work.**

Wow, what a way to smack me round the face, Seth. I'm taking part in Godin's online course, The Marketing Seminar, at the moment, and for you to feel the truth of that statement you might need a few more of his ideas.

A good place to start might be the old marketing maxim that 'no one wants a 3/4-inch drill bit, they want a 3/4-inch hole'. But Godin takes it further – in The Marketing Seminar and in his latest book, *This Is Marketing*. He tells it something like this: people don't want a 3/4-inch hole, they want eight of them. Except they don't want eight holes, they want the shelf that they can put up if they drill eight holes. Except they don't want that; what they want is for their stuff to be on the shelf and not on the floor.

Except they don't want that, they want a tidy room. Except they don't want that, they want the feeling they get when they walk in that room: that their life is in order, that they have things under control, that everything is organised and settled and good.

So don't market them a 3/4 inch drill bit, market them the feeling of their life being organised and settled and good.

This idea isn't obvious but understanding it makes it easier to understand something else important, too: **people who buy something believe they get more value from having it than from the money they pay for it**. Otherwise, why would they swap their money for the thing? This gets interesting when you think about charitable giving, especially of large amounts. The question is: why would someone give thousands or even millions of pounds away? Well, that's the question of someone who (like me) has never felt what it's like to give away thousands or millions of pounds to a worthy cause. Philanthropists give money away because they get more from giving it away than they do from having it.

On a small scale, I've found this to be true as I upped my charitable giving in the last couple of years. It's not as much as I could give (almost no one in a country like the UK gives that) but it's way more than I've ever given before. And I feel better. That's the benefit I get. I feel like my worldview is tight, like I'm within integrity, like I'm doing something to contribute to the cause I feel is most important in the world in the most effective way I can with my money (for me, it's extreme poverty, mainly in North Africa, via GiveDirectly).

There's also a little corollary here about empathy: it's hard, as someone calling potential donors, to get them to give millions of pounds. Part of the reason it's extra hard is because most people *don't understand why someone would give away millions of pounds*. And that makes sense: most people have never had millions of pounds, let alone given that kind of money away. It really helps to develop deep empathy for your customers, because then you can start to speak to the beliefs and parts of them that just might give you their money. Eagle-eyed readers will see that this transfers across industries: if you're a travel agent, book some holidays for yourself, find out what it's like. If you're a doctor, make sure you go to the doctor. If you're a coach, hire yourself a coach. Right now.

But wait, what does this have to do with stealing? Well, here's the thing. First, you need to trust that people buy from you because they get more value than they are paying, and that their experience or product is worth more to them than the cash. And let's give 'people' some credit here: let's not presume they're all manipulated by sleazy marketers or salespeople. Let's assume they're sensible, thoughtful people like you and I, doing the best they can to make the right decisions with their money and getting it right most of the time (and let's remember that you and I aren't sleazy marketers; we're people doing good work that we believe will make the world better). If people are getting more than they pay, then by selling to them you are actually giving them more than they had. That's the magic of trade, that we both end up better off (because, say, you value my book more than £8.99 in cash in the bank, and I value some cash in my bank account more than a copy of my book).

If you don't market your work, you can't sell it. If you can't sell it, people can't buy it. If they can't buy it, they can't be better off by having it. So they are worse off. Not everyone, of course, is worse off if you don't market your work...but those few people who *really want what you have*, are. And those people, those are the ones who matter the most.

So stop stealing, and start talking about your work.

Chapter Ten

You Have a Responsibility To Share And To Share Carefully

Written on 21st August, 2019

I was thinking this week about the awesome power of the Internet to spread wonderful things. I was lying in bed with my wife, listening to a playlist of the songs that were the table names at our wedding a year ago. They are all beautiful pieces of songwriting, holding within them – in our eyes – all the beauty and tragedy of love. And what a wonderful thing it is that we can create that playlist and listen to it. More than that, what a wonderful thing that if we want we can share it with others, then they can experience the curation that Emma and I did after lifetimes of listening to music at our best times and our worst times and everything in between.

Not only that, but I can create another playlist featuring all the songs from our wedding: the readings, the table names, the songs that were played live by us, our family and our friends, and even the song we danced to together in the traditional first dance.

And I can share that with people, sharing those beautifully expressed sentiments of love and life with others who may not know the beauty of these particular bits of songwriting by John Lennon, Brandi Carlile, Gill Landry, Noel Gallagher and others. I can share it here, on Facebook, via WhatsApp, via all these amazing platforms, sending more love and beauty and depth of human understanding out into the world.

But of course that's not all that happens via the incredible power of the Internet to connect us to each other. Facebook's original mission was 'make the world more open and connected'. 'How could that be anything other than good?' we thought.

But *everything* has a light side and a shadow. And what happens when everyone is connected is not only that we have the opportunity to share beautiful pieces of songwriting with each other, but that we have the opportunity to say horrible things to each other anonymously. It turns out that being massively connected leads to lots of people saying really awful things. Racism has reared its head again in English football again this week, with players and managers calling for more work to be done by social media companies to prevent this kind of thing happening. The social media companies, though, are caving under the strain of their sudden responsibility: how do they ban people? Is it their job to protect free speech? Are they the right people to have the responsibility for censorship? Is it moral to remove someone from Facebook because of their political views, for example, when Facebook now holds such a vital place in society as a communication method? Would you remove someone's access to a telephone line because of their political views?

These are the kind of impossible decisions that social media companies – and governments – are currently wrestling with.

And what, might you ask, does this have to do with me sharing a playlist of songs about love? Well, I believe each of us has a responsibility in our online interactions. Each of us has more connection and more opportunity to find an audience than anyone at any earlier point in human history. With more people around the world connecting to the Internet every day, that last sentence has probably been true every day of this millennium and probably will be true for many years to come.

With that opportunity comes responsibility. In order to steady the ship we are all on together, each and every one of us has a responsibility to make a contribution. To share the things we have created. But also to decide: am I sharing something that will make the world better? Am I sharing something that will make the world worse? Does this comment help? Does it hurt? Does it come from the wisdom and skill of the higher parts of us or the vindictive, baser parts of us?

Each of us has that responsibility in every moment. Social media companies are struggling with their responsibility and governments are struggling with theirs. And I hope they all deepen their understanding and come up with solutions to help. But what I *know* will make a difference right here, right now, is if each of us takes more responsibility. So each day, make your decisions. Decide to be a part of the solution to the challenges of polarisation and separation and division in the world. Decide each day *not* to be part of the problem.

You have a responsibility to share your work: to create it and to share it to make the world better. But you also have a responsibility to share carefully and wisely. To be, as much as you can, the person you are on your best days.

Chapter Eleven

Why You Owe It To The People You Know To Share Your Voice

Written on 6ᵗʰ July, 2018

Sometimes, I feel like the lone different voice in the echo chamber of my Facebook feed. Mostly, I find it too frightening to post the thoughts that make me feel like that, frightened of people disliking me, or unfriending me, or something. And sometimes I do post them. I posted one this morning. A different voice to what 'everyone else' is saying.

Also this morning I was listening to Malcolm Gladwell's podcast. It's as brilliant as his books. I love the way he brings together his fantastic eye for something that doesn't make sense and his awesome storytelling to show us things we haven't seen before. Today, I listened to an episode about the idea that the least agreeable people among us can see what the actual best things to do are, even when most of us – because we aren't so disagreeable – may think it is a terrible idea. (In this case, 'agreeable' and 'disagreeable' are terms from psychology describing the key traits people differ on.) Because he's Malcolm

Gladwell, he uses ice hockey and a home invasion movie to demonstrate this. In the latter, the best thing to do with a psychopath in your home threatening your children – the only way to improve your survival chances and those of your children – is to run away, leaving your children with him. This is because either he's going to kill them anyway, or he is not going to hurt them if you leave because you're not there anymore and so there's no point hurting them. Either way, running for help is the only way to save some or all of you. Now most of us, because we can't be this cold (disagreeable) about things like this, couldn't make that decision. We couldn't leave our spouse or children in the hands of Evil Idris Elba (in this particular movie), because it's just not human to do that. But by staying with them, we stay at a 0.5 per cent chance of survival (let's say) rather than giving everyone a six per cent chance of survival (let's say) by running and leaving them. How is this the way to look after our children? It's certainly not rational.

I have worked in some of the most humane and 'agreeable' sectors – arts, charities, and now coaching – full of people with incredible empathy (often the really 'disagreeable' people don't have that at all) and incredible care for people. And I have done this because I have this too: I can understand people deeply and feel deeply. It's one of my strengths. And yet there's another strength, too.

When I was 14, we had standardised tests at school. I scored top in my year in maths. I think I scored 117 (not out of 100 but if I remember right – and I find it hard to believe this – I think out of 120). This was at a new, bigger school, and I knew something was up at that point. There was something I could do here that others couldn't do. And maths is about engaging rationality and persistence and finding *the right answer*.

These days, I don't think about that much. But today, I did. Because if I believe so much (and I do) in a strengths-based approach – that the way to improve the world for ourselves and everyone else is to do the work that we are uniquely suited to do, to find our zones of genius and create from there – then I can't ignore this.

My brother once showed me a rather unsettling clip of the psychologist Jordan Peterson, whose work includes research on those personality traits like agreeableness. He said that we have a responsibility to speak the truth as we see it. We see the world differently from everyone else, and we owe it to everyone to respect what we see, and to share it, rather than hide it away.

Out of about 120 people, I was the best at maths. Only just: someone else, my friend Lindsay, I think, scored only a couple of points less. But I was the best, nonetheless. And I've added all sorts of learning and understanding to myself since then, in rational and less rational places.

It's uncomfortable to feel like the lone voice, but don't I owe it to the people I know to offer the perspective that they may not have seen yet? To give them the choice to see from that perspective if they want to, where they may not have had that choice before? To be my mix of the rational and the emotional, to bring my mix of the search for *the right answer* and my understanding of people? I had a gift that set me apart from most of my classmates, in rationality and persistence and finding the *right answer*. Don't I owe it to them to help them see what I think the right answer is?

You may not have been the best person in your year at maths, but there is a unique mix of strengths and thoughts in your mind that no one else has. Don't you owe it to the people you know to try and help them develop their understanding, by sharing your voice?

I think you do.

Chapter Twelve

You Can't Contribute If You Never Leave Your Room

Written on 29th August, 2019

I love the work of Steven Pressfield. But if there is one idea from Pressfield's incredible non-fiction work that is the most important to remember it is probably this: our inspiration is always there, but it's at the moment when we commit to something and make the start that we let inspiration in.[4]

So, sometimes, sit. And start.

When we start, something changes. We become *someone who can start.*

We create something. From nothing. And, like pushing a car, once the car is moving, keeping it moving is WAY easier. Changing the speed of something is where the force is really needed (that's basic physics). Keeping it moving, that's different.

Starting, no matter how small, can be the most important thing. Then, you have to keep going.

One of the things I was talking to my colleagues at 64 Million Artists about this week is: do you create for the audience, or do you create for yourself?

There are MANY people out there creating only for the audience, consciously or not. The audience on Instagram ('will I get likes?'), the audience on YouTube ('will I get views?'), the audience on LinkedIn ('will I get clicks?').

The thing is, if you are creating for the audience and *only* for the audience, only for the likes or the views or the clicks, then if you don't get those things you have failed. Your effort was wasted. Maybe not quite completely if you have a good frame of learning, but if your measure of success is clicks, then if you don't get clicks what are you left with?

If you are creating just for the sake of creating, that's different. Where true creativity has happened, there is *always* at least one person who is changed: the creator. You can't not be changed by that. My friend Jo Hunter, who founded 64 Million Artists, talks about why empowering people to be creative is so important, how it changes us, in her TEDx Talk.

It's a wonderful thing to change yourself. My work depends on people coming to me and deciding they want to invest their time and their money in changing themselves. And I know that if I help a person change themselves, then that will change their friends, their colleagues, their partner, their children, too. That's the beauty of the world: we are all connected far more than we think.

But the world we live in is an uncertain world. There is division, there is polarisation; things that felt fixed feel fixed no longer; things we thought would last forever don't look so permanent any more. There is – for me at least – an unsettling feeling in the world. Despite my rational optimism (the world is so much better than it used to be in so many ways, why wouldn't that continue?), there's something in the air. We are living through *a time* right now, perhaps particularly in the UK and the USA. Even more than usual, we are living through history.

If this concerns you, then my challenge to you is this: changing yourself is *necessary*, but it is not *sufficient*. Given the times we live in, the complexity of the world and the opportunity of the Internet age, it is vital that each of us who are capable of it changes others. Change people through *the way you are:* by being the most kind, tolerant, thoughtful, skilful, wise, courageous person you can. And, change them through *what you create*.

And don't let Resistance stop you sharing. You are probably a bad judge of how useful the things you have created are for other people. Don't create *only* for others. But, make a contribution.

You can't contribute if you never leave your room.

And your work can't contribute if you never share it.

Note

4   I thought and told people for many years that this was a direct quotation of Steven Pressfield. But I had an unsettling and quite funny discovery when checking the quotation for How to Start When You're Stuck: although this idea is in The War of Art, this is not something written by Pressfield, it is something written by me!

Chapter Thirteen

The Heroes Are The Ones Who Do It Anyway

Written on 6th December, 2018

I was reading back through some of my old articles this week. When I send something out to my mailing list I include – because I now have over 100 articles, plus other videos and different pieces of work available – an 'in case you missed it' section. I wanted to choose an old piece I'd written. When I looked back at some of those early pieces, I realised just how much better my writing is now than it was two-and-a-bit years ago when I started writing pieces in 12 minutes, then always on my train journey.

I didn't really judge myself for that change, because of course that is one of the powerful things about a regular practice. Not only do you create a body of work, but also you improve. If it's a writing practice, not only does your writing improve, but your thinking does too.

And then I was reminded why it's important to share our work, even if we aren't proud of it. And why it's important to leave it out there, even if we think it's not nearly as exciting as what we can create now.

One of the first longer pieces of writing I published was one about Resistance, the force we have to fight in our creative battles, which tries to keep us small and keep us from the things that – deep down – we are called to and desire. I originally wrote it in response to a request from someone for guest posts for their blog, but they didn't use it, and after a while I started to think: 'Maybe this somehow is Resistance. *I need to get it out.*' So I did.

One of the people who commented on it was my friend Paul Thompson. He works – for now at least – in public health, doing important work in the Lancashire borough where he lives. Something about the article resonated with him and – as I remember it – within a few days he had done something he'd been meaning to do for a while: started his own business. The message in the article was clear: you'll feel Resistance, you'll always have reasons not to take the steps. *But you need to take them anyway.*

This week I've been reflecting on that, because Paul handed in his notice. From next year, he will be working full time on PT Health Coaching. And while I know he has done valuable work in his role at the council I am also confident that, freed to be entrepreneurial and follow his spark in his own business, his impact will be even greater, helping people look after themselves, and organisations look after their people. I'm happy for him, and I'm pretty sure that he will be happier and create the money and lifestyle that he wants from taking this step. That's exciting, and I feel like I was a part of that. The world will – for Paul and the wider community – be at least a little better when he is freed to have a greater impact through the vessel of his own business. And what more than that could we really hope for: that the world is a little better tomorrow than it was today?

But it got me thinking again, about Resistance. And about the importance of sharing our work. I had so much Resistance about that article on Resistance. I haven't looked at it for a long time, despite linking to it in articles when I mention the concept, because I don't feel like my writing is as good there as it is now. More than that: *the ideas aren't even mine.* But none of that matters, because – even if the *only* impact it had was on Paul, and even if in reality that was a *tiny* impact – sharing that article was work well done. Putting that out there was a good day.

So remember: there are no new ideas, so don't get tied up in being original. Just share it.

Remember: the only thing we can really hope for is to make the world a little better today than it was yesterday, in some small way, and do the same again tomorrow. So make it better.

Remember: you only need to impact one person today, in a tiny way, to potentially change the course of their life, and their family after that, and who knows what else, forever. So make the impact.

Remember: it doesn't have to be perfect, and the You of Tomorrow will probably be better at it than the You of Today anyway, so there's no point trying to be perfect. You can't compete with You of the Future, so stop worrying and get it out there.

Remember: Resistance will always be there. You won't always feel like it. You'll be scared. You'll doubt yourself. But the heroes? The heroes are the ones who do it anyway.

Chapter Fourteen

Let's Create A New World, The World We All Dream Of

Written on 30th November, 2017

Here I am. I sit here and wait. I sip a coffee. I open myself to you. And this is what you say. Through me.

There is a god. There is more than just us. There is something out there. Something more than the rational mind. Something more.

It speaks through me, when I let it. It would speak through you, if you let it. It speaks in poems, in stories, in dance. It speaks in music, in paintings, in creation. It has spoken through me in many ways, over the years.

A 14-line rhyming poem, to a friend, which 'expressed more than 20 emails'. The lyrics to an unfinished song, sent to my love, which told her the story of how she had found and saved me. Which said it in a way that otherwise I could not have said. My creation has never been a thinker's creation. At that point the magic is gone. My creation has always been through me, not by me. Has always come from somewhere else. Somewhere deep inside. Somewhere definitely outside.

I open myself to you, now, inspiration. I open myself to you, muse. I open myself to you, God, though I don't believe in you.

Come to me, children, and let's play. Let's play in this grand world we live in. Let's take it on and take it over. Let's create a new world, the world we all dream of. How do we do that? We open to the creative spirits we are. We allow them out, through the cynicism and the fear, through the doubt and the judgment. We bring love where we go and then everything changes.

When the creative child is released, we are no longer critical. We are no longer tied to ourselves. We are no longer feared. We see our fear for what it is: the thing that allows us to be brave. Because, children, we are brave. It is brave to open ourselves to what we are really capable of. To allow things out from inside us. To allow that there is something inside us. To allow that there is more than us.

That there is a difference between what we see and what we know. What we think and what we know. What we know and what we *can* know, if we let ourselves.

There is a deep wisdom within us. It will speak, if we can let it. It comes from within us, and it *knows*. It comes from outside us, from above us, from beneath us, from around us. And it *knows*.

It will guide us, and it will lead us, and we will lead it, and we will lead you. We will lead you, children, who cannot yet lead yourselves. We will lead you to the place where you can expand, and grow, and contract to your essence, and know why. We will lead you, children, who cannot yet lead yourselves.

We are the brave. We are the creators. We are the children who will never grow up, though we grow old. We are the heroes who lead the charge. The heroes who hold the pass. For though the world is a world of wonders, for though the march of progress and prosperity is a marvel, for though we must bring the magic of the world of connection to all... For all that, we must hold the pass. We must hold it for honour and valour, for love and acceptance, for the strong and the weak, for the smiles and the tears. We must hold it for the chance to hold our child as she smiles. For the chance to hold our parent as he passes. We must hold it for the connection, through which we will guide you into this new world. The new world. The world that doesn't look back, and doesn't look forward. The world that embraces all that was, light and dark, for each of us and all of us together. The world that stands up to the darkness with ferocious violence and with love. The world that welcomes the unredeemable to their end, with love. The world that embraces the redeemable and, with love, guides them to you, inspiration. To you, creativity. To you, love.

We must hold the pass. We must smile at strangers. We must offer our help. We must never forget our friends. We must hold the pass.

I sit here, and open myself to you, inspiration. To you, muse. To you, God of Creation, though I don't believe in you.

And here is what you say:

You, sitting there, with the sun warming your fingers. Yes, you. You know who I am. You know where I come from. You know I have spoken through all your heroes, in their books, in their songs, in their words of wisdom. I am here and I am real. I am real and I am everywhere. I am here as the feeling rises in your chest and the tears tickle your eyes. I am here in the monologue and the marriage proposal.

I am here in the rational wisdom, which guides you here and guides you there. But I am most here when you release that. When you release your carefully guarded fear, the one you pretend to others and yourself you have broken. When you transcend and include your fear, your Resistance, your former self. When you take him, and care for him, and release him, finally, to allow yourself through. The real you, the beautiful you. The you underneath. The new you.

I am here when you release that little boy, the one in tights in the garden, the one with the shopping basket, the one with the fierce eyes and the quiet sadness. Release him, let him pass on. And release him, let him out now. I am here when you release the tangled teenager, the one with hormones askew, and judgment trapped. The lonely one. The one with elbows everywhere, physically, mentally and emotionally. The lonely one. Release him, let him pass on. And release him, let him out now.

I am here when you release the broken-hearted young man. Lonely again, trapped by judgment, tangled disloyalty. The one opening himself to the new possibilities, to new strengths, to new consciousness. Release him, let him pass on. And release him, let him out now.

You, sitting there, the sun warming your fingers. You are bigger than you know. And you are smaller than you know. But then you know this, deep down. Somewhere, you see this paradox. For you can make no difference. And yet, nothing can make a difference except you. And you. And you. And you. You can each make no difference, and yet no one can make a difference but each of you.

So come to me, children. Come to me and live. Come to me, and feel the feeling that you know. You recognise it. You recognise it from childhood, from first love, from last love, from those moments. You know the ones. Remember them. Savour that feeling. Come to me. Feel the power you have. Feel the source flowing through you. Feel the sense of magic that is deep within you.

Open yourself to me.

Remember this. Remember that this is the place. The still point. Here, the dance is. Where past and future are gathered. Where angels of the past speak through you, where angels of the future await you. Where, without you, there may be no more angels. You may be the last, unless you speak. Unless you speak with your voice. Unless you speak your truth.

For you can make no difference, and yet no one can speak but you. And you. And you. And each of us can make no difference, yet if none of us speaks there will be no more angels. There will be no more love. The pass will fall. And the hordes will advance.

Open yourself to me.

Stand with me, here. On this hillside. Stand with me, here. In this pass. Stand with me here, in this coffee shop, bus stop, country park, forest at dark. In fear and in inspiration. Here must be the stand. The stand for all we believe in. The stand for a better world. The stand for a better life, for each of you and all of you.

Stand with me, here. In this office. Stand with me, here. On this train. Stand with me here, on this wooden bench, wedding tent, song line, moment in time. In love and in desperation. Here must be the stand. The stand for all you believe in. The stand for all of your world, good and bad. The stand for a life and an impossible dream, for each of you and all of you.

Here. Here is what I say.

* * *

I can feel the power rising in me. I seek it from outside. I seek it through the chemicals in my blood and the vitamins in my food. But I find it inside, and in the great outside. And this is different. It is rising in me, from somewhere else. As I sit here, and I open myself.

And even as I do this, the thoughts rise in my mind. I push them down. I breathe. I look through the glass, over the keyboard. At tyres and vans, at children and clouds. I notice the rush of the chemicals – what if this is just them talking? What if there is no inspiration? There is no power? And yet there is. Because I can't remember what I have written. Everything has been building to this point. Every 12-minute piece of writing, every fantasy novel. Every coaching session. Every kiss. Every broken relationship. Every song. Every poem. Every conversation. Every email. Every struggle. Every laugh. Every breath taken. In, and out. Every sound heard, every tear shed. Every moment. Leading to this one. All I can do now is release this, this writing, this laughter. This flow of inspiration.

For it must be released, though the fear rises in me. It must be heard. For the pass must be held. The children must play. And we must listen. We must all listen. And we must act. And we must continue acting. Even when the best action is to sit, silently. By ourselves, or at an easel, or at a keyboard, or at a piano. And wait.

Wait for you, inspiration. Wait for you, muse. Wait for you, God, who I do not believe in.

Wait for the power, wait for the source, wait for the flow of that feeling that we know, so well, when we listen. So open. And wait.

* * *

I feel the flow subsiding now. Or is it the chemicals? Or am I closing myself to you?

Where did this come from? It came from everywhere, and nowhere. It came from everything and nothing. It is the clarity and silence we seek, and it is the roiling storm that we fear.

I open myself, now. And I wait. And I feel love. For the yawning man. For the straining mother. For the woman, at her desk, who is mine and I hers. For the boy, and the teenager, and the young man, and the less young man, now sitting at a keyboard, smiling to himself. You have done well, man and mother, woman and less young man. You have done your best.

So sit, sometimes, and open yourself. You deserve it.

Afterword

Written on 16th September, 2022

The experience of reading that final chapter has an otherworldly quality to me. More than anything else I have ever written, I don't know who wrote it. More than anything else I've ever written, it felt like it emerged through me, rather than being created by me.

And I nearly didn't share it in the first place.

And all the way through the process of thinking about this book I have doubted whether it should go in.

Until I read it today, just before writing this. I cried afterwards.

Of course it goes in.

And the rest of that, the doubt, that's all fear and Resistance.

That's what this journey is like, though. The journey to be all we can be and have all the impact we can have.

The journey to tilt our inner world and the outer world towards heaven and away from hell.

It's full of fear and procrastination and Resistance. Or, at least, it is for me.

Every time I do something new I have to grow in a new way.

The good thing is, though, that when you've consciously grown once, the next time is sometimes easier. At least, then, you know a little about what's on the other side.

That's what happened for me with sharing my work.

Each time I did it, the next time got a bit easier.

Until I levelled up again and wrote about something that tapped into more of my insecurity, that showed more of who I am. When I did that, the procrastination (and the fear behind it) was back.

Each time I've been scared about what I might share, and then shared it, the worst hasn't happened. Even when I have had some kickback in the comments (incredibly rarely – I can only really remember it once) it hasn't been as bad as I imagined.

And in the long term, I think even going through that changed me for the better. It forced me to *really think* about what I believed in. And after I'd done that, I knew.

But over time, I have developed a low tolerance for the nonsense stories I tell myself. I can spot them more easily now for what they are, and then choose to ignore them.

And I have developed an increasing belief in the power of courage. Courage requires fear. And it is one of the most admirable of human qualities.

To be courageous, to do that wonderful, inspiring action, we have to be afraid. Otherwise there is no courage.

To grow, and fulfil our potential, to do what is most important for our souls, we have to do what we are most afraid of.

And when we do, all kinds of amazing things are possible. And all kinds of amazing things may happen.

This practice, which started from facing my fear and sharing things anyway, has certainly changed me.

And that has continued through this series.

The sometimes fear-filled action of changing my identity to include 'author'.

The transformations in me from setting myself a challenge to appear on 100 Podcasts in a year so that I could talk about this kind of work.

These things have cemented just how impactful the decision to face my fear in 2016 was.

I keep learning from that process. I keep seeing more things that have come from it.

That is what is possible, when we look for the places we have the most Resistance, trust Steven Pressfield that they are the most important places for our soul's evolution, and then use that as a compass to choose what to do next.

That raises a question for me, in this moment. Where do I go next? Where is the Resistance the strongest? What am I afraid of and where am I procrastinating?

To grow, perhaps, in scale? To create more partnerships? To say No even more precisely and thoughtfully? Or to say yes: to free myself from the bonds of goals and open myself to possibility?

Sometimes, the answers come easy. In 2016, there were many places I was afraid or wrapped in worry and Resistance. In 2022, there are fewer. And that is true for me because of the number of times I have chosen courage.

That's what I wish for you.

I want to read your book.

I want to know about your business.

I want to listen to your podcast.

I want the change that you want to happen.

I want it for you and I want it for all of us.

It will take courage; no doubt about that.

The courage to risk things. The courage to change who you are.

And the you of now won't like that. Because she or he won't get through that transition alive.

But the bigger you, the higher you, the wiser you. You know that you will come out of that transformation as more than you were before.

And you might just make a little dint in the world while you do it.

Help Spread the Word

I believe that the world is a better place when people are creating things; when people move out of the hell of procrastination, make things that make a difference and then share them.

If you agree with me, or if this book has helped you, please help someone else share their work by doing one of two things:

1. Review this book on Amazon

It really can't be overstated how important reviews are to help a book reach the people it's intended to help. If you have taken something positive from reading this book, please spare five minutes of your time to help someone else find their something positive too. You never know where it might take them.

Even just a rating and one sentence will make a big difference.

2. Tell someone about this book

Do you know someone who always talks about the book they'll write or the business they'll start or the creative project they've just thought of? Maybe they never start. Or maybe they start, finish, but never share it.

If you do, tell them about this book. Tell them the story of how I wrote it. Share the story with them on social media. See if it sparks a conversation. Give it to them for their birthday or for Christmas. It might be exactly what they need.

The world will be transformed by the creativity of ordinary people like you and me. Let's help others unlock their potential and make work that counts.

We're all in this together; let's make it beautiful.

The Cutting Room: Free eBook

This is a book about sharing our work. In it, I've written about how I'm not a good judge of whether the things I make are impactful or not. And that's why I want to share *The Cutting Room* with you.

It's a short eBook that contains those articles I wrote over the first three years of the 12-minute blog that didn't make it into this series of books. Some of them felt like they weren't relevant to a series about finally doing the things we want to do; some overlapped too much with other chapters that did make the books.

But I can't be sure of what will be impactful, and I want to share ALL of my work, just in case it makes a difference.

So if you want a copy of *The Cutting Room* for free, visit **www.robbieswale.com/12minute-method-downloads** or scan this QR code:

We have to live our values, and I believe that it's worth sharing the work we have done, no matter what we think of it, in case just one person is changed by that.

So here's *The Cutting Room*. If you are changed by it, I'd love to know.

Stay Up to Date About The 12-Minute Method

This is the fourth in a series of books, created to support you through the creative process.

To be the first to hear about future books, other 12-Minute Method developments, and my other work, sign up to my mailing list at:

www.robbieswale.com/mailing-list

Acknowledgements

Written on 23rd September, 2022

Ok, here goes. 12 minutes to acknowledge the other people who have made this book possible.

To express gratitude for the people without whom I couldn't or wouldn't have done this work.

It feels extra pressured, because this is the last acknowledgements section in the series. No time to come back and thank people next time! But that's life.

First, there are the people who have practically made this book happen.

Steve Creek, for the conversation in Doppio in Battersea and for the tricky editing work I asked of him: to edit *and* to leave imperfection.

Stefan and his team at Spiffing Covers, for their work on this book and the rest of the series.

There are people who helped earlier in the process: many test readers, including Joni Zwart, who gave great feedback and shared her knowledge of the publishing industry. Tim Pettingale and Joseph Alexander worked on earlier books in the series and helped me find a place for my writing in the often-confusing publishing world. Tim also coined the phrase, 'The 12-Minute Method'.

Jericho Writers was a valued wealth of information to help navigate the publishing industry, too.

Other people have read these books in their various forms, including most recently Alex Swallow, Michael Hubbard, Alex O'Neill and Nadine Kelly. Thank you.

Thanks to the thinkers and authors whose work has inspired the chapters in this book. There are too many to name here, but I stand on the shoulders of many giants.

Thanks to the clients who I have worked with, who played with me in the space of making happen the things they want, including using the ideas in this book. You have taught me so much.

Thanks to the coaches and mentors who have supported me, in particular Mike Toller, Rich Litvin, Katie Harvey, Robert Holden and of course Joel Monk. Support from all of you has been key in me becoming who I am today. But, Joel, the moment when we created the sharing practice, the train series, is one I suspect I'll remember forever. The impact of that (and all the other support I've received at different stages with making these books a reality) will ripple on and out. Once the work is shared, we never know how far it will go.

Thank you to all the heroes who have done it anyway. I mention Paul Thompson in the penultimate chapter of the book, and that is a really meaningful story to me, one that touches my heart. But you can read about other heroes who did it anyway in the 'Impact' section at the start, and there are many, many more who I have had the privilege to work with. There are more still, who have commented on my writing, written reviews on Amazon or sent me messages to tell me about the impact of my work. When I slow down to think, I know that even just one person makes sharing the work worth it, but hearing the stories of how that has happened is such a valuable thing in keeping me going, in reminding me of the importance of sharing my work. There are too many to name all the people who have read and supported the 12-minute blog over the years, but Colin D Smith deserves a special mention: his always-thoughtful comments often came at times when I thought no one was listening, and his support as a thinking partner has been incredibly valuable to me. Thank you.

Thank you to those people I love the most.

To my oldest friends and a WhatsApp group that reminds me always of the possibility of technology to strengthen relationships and bring us together.

To my growing family: mother, father, brother, sister, partners, nephew. Our conversations and your support mean so much to me. They are what life is about.

To Leah: a little dynamo who enriches my life and makes it more meaningful. I can't help but wonder what you'll make of all these things when you're old enough to read them.

To Emma: I love you. Thank you for everything. Words are not enough.

How I Wrote a Book in 12 Minutes: Notes About the Process

For those who are interested, I wanted to add a few words about how this book was created, and the idea of creating a book in 12 minutes, to supplement what I described in the introduction and throughout the book. I share this to give those among you who want to do something similar the power to choose how you do that.

I originally imagined that this series would simply be a compilation of the pieces as they were posted online, but once something starts to become a book (or a series of books), some extra decisions need to be made.

First, it felt important to give myself a little more leeway than I do with the articles when they first go online. I gave myself an extra proofread of the whole book and then sent it to my friend, Steve Creek, a professional copy editor, to give it a once-over.

The spirit of those edits was to improve it, so it could support people even more. It was to tighten and clarify. The substance of the articles was not changed significantly – a sentence was added or removed here and there, a few titles made more relevant or punchier. There were a few tweaks to make the language and sense clearer, or to fix bits that were hazy on detail because the original was written in 12 minutes and there wasn't time to look up precisely what someone had said. After the book came back from Steve, there was some broader feedback and some rearranging of the pieces. Then it sat, pretty much untouched, for about two years (more on that another time).

When I came back to it, with the help of self-publishing entrepreneurs Tim Pettingale and Joseph Alexander, we realised it would work even better as a series. That required another edit from me, again leaving the substance but tightening and making clearer a sentence here and there, or adding a few words or a couple of sentences to make it clear why a particular piece belonged here, in this part of the book or series.

As the publishing process went on, the book received another edit from Steve and another two reads and light edits from me. I noticed, as each time passed, that I was more willing to tweak for clarity and impact, and to more firmly place a piece where it sat in the book. But, as you can tell from reading, these pieces are absolutely imperfect, and many are pretty much the same as when they were originally written on the train or with the 12-minute timer.

At different stages, a few other sections (like this one) were added to tie the book together as a book. Those are the only bits not originally written in 12 minutes, although with most of them, I still set the timer to make sure I got out of my own way and got going. That's how I work. The 12-Minute Method section at the start was written using the timer, but I had to reset it four times to have time to say everything that needed saying (The 48-Minute Method!). The final chapter, as I mentioned near the start of the book, was written in one sitting, but without a timer. But it felt right to place it here in this book anyway.

A few pieces from the series of articles didn't quite belong in a series about creating what you are called to create, so those were removed. Remarkably few pieces from the first three years of the writing practice overlapped in content enough that a piece needed to be removed, but there were a couple, so they came out. I felt that a few more didn't help the flow of the books, so they came out too. This process was surprisingly hard, but it served the books to remove them. All these pieces can be read on LinkedIn where they were originally posted, or on my website, or in a short eBook called *The Cutting Room*, available at:

www.robbieswale.com/12minute-method-downloads

I wasn't sure where to draw the line with which set of 12-minute articles would make up the series, but on my original deadline to send the 'book' to Steve I realised it was three years and one day since I started the weekly practice (after the initial five pieces). So, what makes up this book and the other three in the series are the five original parts of The Train Series and almost exactly three years of weekly articles.

And that, pretty much, is how you write a book (or four!) in 12 minutes.

Manufactured by Amazon.ca
Bolton, ON

34083373R00059